McDynasty

from the ming dynasty to McDonald's

❖

basil dillon-malone

❖

Belfast
LAPWING

First Published by Lapwing Publications
c/o 1, Ballysillan Drive
Belfast BT14 8HQ

British Library Cataloguing in Publication Data.
A catalogue record for this book is available from
the British Library.

Set in Aldine 721 BT
by
Winepress Services

ISBN 1-905425-07-4

CONTENTS

McDynasty

from the ming dynasty to McDonald's

❖

basil dillon-malone

VAGABOND

wasn't it *key largo*
where i searched for
humphrey bogart
at the sheraton
or just the glamour
of the moment

and wasn't it *el cid*
in mazatlan
where the tide at night
rushed to my feet
receding
in imprints
of your footprints

at copacabana
i watched the prettiest girls
in thongs, only
in buenos aires
i listened to the tango
in the rainy night
waiting for you
in santiago i became
latino

in tel aviv i saw my dream
at the pool
i could smell your perfume
of course you were a
reflection

in cairo the worry-beads
were someone else's
not the princess's
not even when your hegab fell
slapped by the zealot,
you are too proud

in beijing that single line
in mandarin
was my encyclopedia
in taipei it was your smile
in tokyo it was
how you asked my name

in hong kong you were
on the mountain peak
overlooking the universe
in montreal and new orleans
it was an *old town* accent
from another continent

in dublin, london, paris, zurich
a stream of consciousness
was my incurable hope

>   *if i ever found you in the*
>   *loud lighthouse glare*
>   *as it passed you were lost*
>   *in the silence of on ocean*

in a hundred other cities
and tonight in bonnie castle
i have searched for you

>   *mumtaz*

queen of the taj mahal

soon i will know if you are

>   real

GOLDEN ARCHES

museum room in the ray kroc plaza

there's a sixth-floor room
in oakbrook
fernando showed it to me
without permission
you can unwind
for twenty-minutes
if you work there
or really just unload
if the missus
or
my old man gets me down

the walls unfold
with pastel carpet-panels
you can even write poetry
for a while

there's another room
shaped like a flying saucer
you can lie on a cushioned
floor and listen
to beethoven's fifth in
quadraphonic cubed in
pitch-darkness really pitch and
set the dials to your
taste of buttons

and another room

with ray kroc's undisturbed
cup of coffee when he died
or you can listen to him talk
of any subject

even using four-letter-words

videotaped from every talk-show
over twenty-years

a touch-panel on a screen
retrieves in eight-seconds
online-flat any queried-word
he spoke

a simple task
for 4 IBM 3090's turbo
as a lightning stroke

there's another room
in 10000 stores
in six continents
in a hundred countries
in a thousand cities where
a billion people come to fare
ubiquity draws them there
intuitively

to a yellow room
where coffee isn't scalding [1]

     i preferred

---

[1] *scalding-coffee lawsuit gave rise to escalating frivolous-litigation industry*

AUSSIE ARCHITECTURE

opera house outlandish
upclose
unlike postcards
of strange shapes only
it goes on and on
in chambers
by the sydney seasound

shell by shellroof
each mammoth section
a symphony
kind of call
to the impossible
urgeness
of blinding deafness
when unreal surreal sonics
heard

      or seen

in seashells
close to your ear

faraway
things are different

      than sounds

maestro's way to manifest
bigness from smallness
neither is
hollow or shallow

architect,
performer, composer
composure
in this dishshell

ASIAN RHYTHM

she dances
like a rhyme in a lyric
never takes her eyes
from the

                   floor

is sparkling
in kaleidoscop ic

my eyes follow reaching
hers
are right and left
converging for a

                   ... sec

ond ...

seems infinite when
from midnight until four
she comes to disco
with her eyes upon the

                   floor

her patent
highheeled squareheeled
shoes are silent
her long gown
sideslit at her hip, almost
revealing

                   now and

then

click click her fingers
attract attention
like the

                   nod of her head

shaking

her long dark hair

                   tossing

covering
her toopainted face

SOMEWHERE ELSE

did you ever dream
that you were alone
and you were
and the mist was high
in the morning
or low in any
graveyard
i
often think
of hidden things and
what you are thinking

perhaps it is of
me

the sea is wide and even
blackbirds hibernate
in some distant climate
because they
too
suffer from an urge
floating
like a particle
of dust
in the apocalypse

some never
return

LONER
   AND A BAR-ROOM MIRROR
          at the harp bar in dublin

he
sits at the bar
fists intertwined
in pyramid knuckles
resting on elbows
staring at dreams
mahogany mirrors
reflected in tumblers
watery eyeballs
and gin

he
comes here to sit
as he stares at himself
and he stares at himself
and his gin
and sooner or later
there's only himself
not the barman, the daydream
or the blame of being
him

LI-*BARRY*

legacy to my son at 13

this too will be yours   (i told him)

young as he was he tried to grasp the hidden wealth
beyond the titles covering a wall 16 feet by 8

these books are part of me

when i'm gone you may know me better
something is here of your dad, grandfather
good, complex, not-unconcealed
that causing rifts among close ones
with more points of view than convergence

my personality's not painted on this wall

perhaps some of it between the painted shelves
like sleeves of a book not adequately sharing
what's inside

when you see me laugh or sad in real life

you'll see reality's not a reaction but an illustration
of what an author may have felt before to influence
not to clone

these words are the world's greatest, worst thinkers

when thought is subjective as a stream-of-consciousness
combine all thoughts, then read your mind
these books are my best friends, occasional enemies —
conflict leads to information, then to being informed

this library's my furniture, it never grows old

not in a glass case or mirrored cage, the door to its
accessibility is curiosity, its secrets aren't hidden
by the transparency of a reflection

these books are a collection

not of coins that can be traded for silver but ideas
to trade for more, share them
with those who will use them not make a case for show —
there are more borrowers (i have learned)
than those who cherish nourishment

nice to look at, like at a pretty woman

don't browse too long, don't loiter, an introduction
can lead to a pleasant friendship
fine to show off there is wisdom in that
a conversation piece if the discussion
becomes not monologues in competition but a conversation

many of these works are of

latin and greek, hebrew and islam, as much as
technology of sega, philosophy of space
the space of the universe, my reference
when i need a balance in the excess of life's mediocrity

when you disagree with me

you will have travelled this wall, my legacy to you,
keep it, don't sell it for coins but ideas.
you and your children will be rich as the wealth
of dependable companionship, of discerning discovery

VIVA

1.   i sat on a bench in st. michel
        in the noisy latin quarter
        intermingling with painters and poets
        in monmartre where sartre wrote
        where students clamoured in the sixties
        in the crowded boulevards
        where the artist painted his model
                babette
        whom he would never forget
        and forgot

        in the way that students do
        when i too
        had forgotten
        you

                        i often think of *babette*
                        and your other names

        ah, the students of the sorbonne
        the outlaws of the legion
        the passion the idealism

2.   in the hotel lutetia
        which was hitler's headquarters
        and map-room
        i slept with the devil in paris
        in the city of craft
                        on an eiderdown mattress

        in the dark realism with its deception
        of subconscious imagery
        and when i learned of this war-room
        for his scheme
        a nerve-center nap-room for his dream
        for millions on their mattresses of stone
        in this fortress alone
        the words 'hidden consent'
        seemed credible
        of millions against millions against

        "… the illusion of a loftier reality"
                        (r.w.emerson)

the *laissez-faire* of ovens and ovens
the *savoir-faire* of business as usual
for millions
by millions of the reich as i tossed
        on my eiderdown mattress

3.   and in lyon, and nice,
the sun that burns pale irish
faces that we risk
for glamor
the glamor and the glare
in dreams that we had

4.   the entourage
now moving on
to limoges china
worth nothing
if chipped

and,
when we climbed in the rain
over the hill
when they faked the stalled-bus
       for us tourists
telling us
we had to find our own way
to their destination
       for us

our hosts like children giggled
at their surprise
       for us

as over this hill hiked-out
was the medieval castle
of limoges like a mirage
in the algerian desert

tout-de-suite we were charmed
by the town brass band
playing the star bangled banner
       for us

with dull french humour
patronising their
ingenuousness
dressed like pilgrims
in contrast
to our welcome to france
by mitterand

      with thirty-six greens
      on his lawn
      for his workers' republic

5.   departing from calais
above the chunnel
on a hovercraft we hovered
to the white cliffs

      like flags of surrender

INSOMNIA ...

interrupted darkness
by a flame and strumming
silence and a ticktock
nightmare

she moved through the clouds
shrouding my bed like sheets

had i dreamt of channels
and subterranean caves
where hobos dwell
remembering montmartre
and motion
in a passive night?

lying and waiting
to vanish and forget
and be forgotten

until the leaves have fallen
and withered
like an old man

i am
tomorrow, nicotine rot
silence and a ticktock
nightmare

CONTOURS FROM AN AIRBUS

jigsaw-puzzle over maine, quadrangles in hong kong
crazy quilting landscapes like a random eiderdown
of rolling vales near leitrim with patterns of lace
intergalactic phantoms looking upward into space
while dot-to-dots at nighttime jot together in your mind
croatian landmined limbo calmly staggered to a grind
some shapes are just preposterous, fanciful, alone
some shapes distort the present for the shape of things to come

> *yellow sea is yellow you can see its mellow floor*
> *red sea etches history and opens up no more*

like the epicenter-hole concentric-circle from the cloud
mount fuji's vulcan timidness contrasts the engines loud
ramses fingered delta snakes a nile of potted mosques
midway island's lagoon-atoll bluegreen depth is lost
where asia's front dragged eager drones to allies half-way house
disintegrating literally hiroshima's christ
and shapes and shapes of flats and flats as flat as 2-d squares
are 3-d now again with baseball-diamonds everywhere

> *descending into bangkok watch the buddha temple's gold*
> *not unassuming guangzhou monks, confucius creed of hope*

red rainbow over china comes full circle in the sky
hula-hoop outspoking pots of gold no end in sight
two thousand miles of zigzagged wall through ricewheat paddygrass
dots, or people's foreheads from new delhi to madras
bueno buenos aires there is movement hard to see
lasso-noosing gaucho or the man from laramee
christ redeeming mountain over rio's splendid hue
tell's a shape fulfilling picture of ten million points of view

> *twenty thousand gods above the taj mahal protect*
> *the opulence of raja caste, the alms of past neglect*

kibbutz pegs are scattering into ashen galilee
andes slicing pavements roll a path across chile
obelisk in egypt just a pindot looking down
night-lights dead in peking hoard an escalating yuan
gothic block of big ben's top, flat as a wall street roof
wenceslas square in prague's new past, lost origins of proof
shapes of squares, rectangles, irrigation tilling zones
from thirty-seven thousand feet a painter's etching roams

elliptical, symmetrical, symbolic broken shapes
are hidden by the clouds that hide a soon forgotten face

horizon vast of wilderness, penisular steep hills
deciduous, coniferous sequoia pyramids
laissez faire meandering lake water forms a line
as crooked as the cheating heart that tends to undermine
and isolate boxed countries, now lightning turbulence
forms across the universe with thundering cadence
glistened river sparkles in the red eye of the sun
green eve of the yellow god[1] forever gazes down

newsroom pans atrocities of sarajevon nam
looking down from heaven at a world naively calm

a raincircle, and peace
looking down from 37,000 feet
on a round-the-world ticket with
triple mileage points

1 *Monologue of British-colonial Kathmandu, by J. Milton Hayes*

U.K.

winchester   1.   i remembered the song *winchester cathedral*
in winchester cathedral

in the multilateral presbytery
without its polychromy
in the wake of henry
the eighth's n-th wife

in the square nave
under the ribbed vault of the dome
as i stood over jane austen's tomb
without realizing it

which i wouldn't have done
although it's a cement block in the ground
seeming inappropriate for literature
put to bed

everyone walking on top of jane austen
to the angst of the sacristan's
fiery stare

london   2.   in the *carriage house*
the oldest pub in london
i was skeptical when they told us
that shakespeare too imbibed here

remembering last year
in the shanghai *bosses club*
(a perk for 80-yuan[1]-a-week)
executives excitedly telling us
that marco polo too
dined there -
recently
trying to impress us believing it too
a millennium later

the hifalutin' pub conversation
drawled on with bluffs
and vignettes
in the stuff that stuffed-shirts
and executives love
drinking our pints
which need no justification
in english or any language

chelsea 3. after *cats* i remembered
opening night of *my fair lady*
in '66 in the west end with donna
and being stuck predictably
tn the tube at chelsea
frantic that i'd miss my first real date
when you emigrated from mayo

god help us

never thinking you would let me
take you out and you did

as the chorus left i never saw you again
oh donna. paul anka

oxford 4. the dreaming spires of oxford
where my cousin read
who played the piano
while my brother at home
could only whistle
while another played the melodeon

xiao qian
and cambridge

5. king's college, cambridge
where my now aged friend,
xiao qian, [2]
professor and sage, read *ulysses*
as a research student
and then a war correspondent
for china
with his photo on the cover
of *life* magazine.
he had afternoon tea
with orwell and ryland, both georges

(not bourgeois or gorgeous
like the inelegant georges I and II
wedlocking
english queens becoming
                english kings
with thick german accents mocking the
                king's english
with no interest in
anything english
while philip from greece
at least spoke the *e*lingo
with 'is foot-in-'is-jaw
much of the time
to liz's chagrin
like the foot-and-mouth dilemma
that welcomes you at heathrow)

incarcerated after translating
napoleon into mandarin,
xiao qian, at mao's invitation
anachronistically
reciprocating his intellectualism
paradoxically -

                with ten years on a workers' farm
                myopically
                        taught by jesuits
                to be re-educated on tillage

- the professor, also knew
bertrand russell, virginia woolf,
em forster, hg wells, edgar snow
in england
and drank with hemingway, too,
my journalist friend
who lost a kidney and almost his wife
on the labor farms

                "my life a small sacrifice for china"
                        he wrote
                remembering the english gunboats
                wasting his homeland
                at the turn of the century
                on a slow-boat to china

to wales 6.   the slow-slow train to woking broken
intermittently predictably
to bristol not so far away
from the nuclear power plant in wylva
where on a student tour from dublin
we almost caused the first reaction

drunk as engineering students
extracurricularly
are prone to be predictably
on that all-night pissup
on the choppy irish sea
rolling and rolling feeling nothing
fearing less

        even when matt harley cut my wrist
        and his
        with a penknife
        rubbing sliced-wrists together
        as sloshed blood-brothers
        for the crocked cult of the moment

welch bobbies met us with their jawed stares
and raised hats

        and a good day to you ossifer

and raised batons
in the wales of dylan thomas
emulating behan too

scotland 7.   our honeymoon in edinburgh castle
with my first wife and
the cold kilts,
the streets of glasgow
and children kicking footballs
against walls with glass windows
sharing coal chimneys.
your yorkshire penfriend,
yorkshire pudding,
newcastle lager, alvick castle

the friary 8.   and on the coast nearby
the dilapidated friary
of franciscans-
of-the-strict-observance,
its refectory and dormitory
now nettled with weeds
overlooking the frothy north sea
in the gale force wind

roofless, empty
of titular priors and monks,
its piscina niches for sacred vessels
in the chapel cunningly contrived
in jambs of altar recesses,
a reader's desk in a window niche
for their scriptures in latin
and manuscripts

like the *book of kells* now at *trinity*
and other texts
perpetuating
how the irish saved civilization
        [thomas cahill]

before the expiration of the monks
the books transported in safety
to even remoter monasteries
far far up in the rocky north
from northmen and vikings
invading history

evading mountainous ridges
that the norsemen left behind
seeking fertile land from fjords
seeking greener pastures
seeking monk-rich chalices
apparently
bored in their craggy home
in the lure of effortless conquests
of friars in robes
without daggers hidden
in their cloaks

round tower 9.   you can imagine them now, the monks,
fleeing their assailants
in panic up long slender ladders
up up tripping on their garments,
togas and frocks,
cassocks and other puffy vestments
into the little wicket-gate of their watershed,
of their tall round tower, panoramic
        like glendalough in ireland

pulling the long ladder inside
clumsily
terror-stricken slipping on their skirts
tucking their tushes behind 'em

like nebulae dust particles
trailing the celestial body
of a stellar nomad

        as if the leonid shower
of the tempel-tuttle comet
that streaks across the sky
once each generation
with skirts of orbital debris
of ethereal snowballed
fireballed meteors

        like a truck barreling
down a dirt road
that we watched in the night
in another country
romantically,
staggering white explosions
of a thousand meteors per hour
streaking overhead
leaving saintly
faint trails
behind
'em

the monks
like disciples following their faith
obediently, fearfully, trustingly
desperately
like the *children-of-this-world*

with more faith in corporeal
self-preservation and their leader

      their bellwether-sheep
      shepherding its flock
      first-in in front of 'em,

      than in the faith of spirituality

      and their vows

against the giant northern encroachers,
praying to saint christopher
who carried 'christ' on his shoulders,
patron saint of travelers,
one up
on the ladder,
one up on the invaders

now

from this cloistered abbey,
        conceptualizing all of this
looking across the stormy sea
and the wavy currents of

      "the witness of the times
      the messenger of antiquity"
      [cicero]

and the arguments of nature

birmingham 10.	windsor's book-shelves filled unread
by queens,
birmingham jails reminding me of
birmingham alabama
and martin luther
king
parliamentarians *sent to coventry*

on an order from the
archetypal-divorcé himself
king
henry-8 dissolving papal chapels
and st. john's
filling it with prisoners in 1645
isolated, ignored

sequestered, predictably
other divorces elsewhere on orders
of eviction
without six wives

liverpool 11.	liverpool with more irish than dublin,
the beatles and u2
uk. u2
ok. utoo

oh liverpool lou, lovely liverpool lou
why can't ye behave now like other girls do

written and sung
by brendan (behan)'s brother

liverpudlians playing soccer
in puddles of rain

reigning monarchs in the media
with their families

arundal 12.	a catholic bishop my cousin
with his home in arundal castle

[1] 80-yuan or RMB = $10
[2] member Chinese Writers Assoc, translator *Ulysses* into Mandarin

DECISIONS

insecticidally
as i saw a creepie
crawling
on the floor

my first instinct
was to squash the poor
bugger
into squishisity
until

i put my mind in its own
instinct
oblivious to the
catastrophe
awaiting it

and while i was
rationalizing
all of this
i stepped down hard
on top of it
taking both of us
instinctively
out of our misery

in the
splatology
of another bug's death
which could be
a fatal run-in

with a windshield

or slapping a mosquito
on your cheek
leaving a blood streak
of death and resurrection

watching
love-bugs coming alive

in the rain

copulating in midair
laying eggs
in anything rotten
even mistaking
exhaust fumes for rot
swarming
all over the street
causing car-gunk
in splotches
moths with scales
coming off their wings
insects putting nutrients
back in the soil

mosquitos hatching
male crickets
trying their wings
flying ants taking off
to start new ant hills
here a ladybug a roly-poly
banana spider dragon fly
lace wings leaf hoppers
wasps and grasshoppers
bug fossils
etched on car hoods
sticking to the paint

the point
of all of this
i rationalize
is the natural urge
to live and let live
in nature's course
too late for the
poor bugger

though

whose days are numbered

now
my friend

didn't want to do it
didn't want to do it
the little bugger blew it
crawling on the ground
in front of me
temptingly
blowing in the wind
in my face

   splat!

nothing's either right or wrong
but instinct makes you do it
so much for philanthropy
mortality, morality;

   "a terrible thin covering of ice
   over a sea of primitive barbarity"
   [karl barth]

SUPERBIRD

glancing down
from the 40th storey
of an 80-floor highrise
standing precariously
even on a fenced-in ledge
two feet wide in the high wind
imagining stuntmen

in movies

leaping over railings
like leap-frog ninja turtles
landing on the 39th floor
beneath intact

as you look over and shiver
imagining you're a
daredevil feet-like-putty
(oxymoron) or
margarine that tastes like butter
with jellied knees you wonder
why uninsurable stuntmen
aren't paid like the
pierce brosnans of hollywood

guess not as handsome

for the risks they take
as you lean over
and for a moment imagine
you can fly
have you ever felt like that

for a moment

a seagull now swishing by
skimming your face
for a moment
as large as an albatross
up close
like neil diamond's
jonathan livingston seagull

the movie star stuntbird
instantly passing you by
still fancying you can fly
or riding on its back
like floating on the magic carpet
in the satanic verses
of salmon rushdie
viewing the earth below
now in the distance

as small as a swallow
through opposite lens

binoculars from here
you follow its illogic
flightplan wondering
what **jonnie** would think
of you

cruising on his back

looking over his left wing
at the intruder
the galled seagull bristling
at the stowaway freeloader
gliding through the breeze
like kate and leonardo
in the poster of the titanic
'my heart will go on'

> *git offa*
> *my shoulda*
> *busta!*

(ya chinzy buzzard)

PRIMROSE HILL
listening to father's recitations

*he could suck on the pap of life
and gulp down the incomparable milk of wonder ...*
-ulysses

1.   though never been to kathmandu,
more east than lake lausanne
i saw a vast frontier from
primrose hill
my father's disquisitions
altercations, recitations
entranced me as we slowly
strolled along

grandiloquent and boldly
of a sadly buried past
he conjured up a vision
real, profound
his oozing many tears
at each crescendo
in the wind stifled
its prodigious brief sojourn

a monologue for every lip
to mimic and expound
his monocle contracted
with remorse
dilated with emotion:
throbbing, passion
pain and fear -- his repertoire
flamboyant, debonair

we often sauntered up this path
attended to his tale and stave
and loved him
for the way he gave himself
on primrose hill, walking by the
ditch outside the
sheltered town and down by
attymass

and, babette, too, was there

nine little ducklins
trekking, tripping up the road
intent to hear adage and
anecdote
in veneration to his spell
while the hunter wagged
his drolling tail, and now he lit
his hawthorn pipe

> and years passed by in reverie,
> and we, the sons, grew older,
> and the amulet debutantes and
> mother too
> while the winding stretch
> could not divert its frequent route
> rebuking time its vatic right,
> above the town

>> and he harangued parlance,
>> contrived an epic

the neighbors thought it all archaic,
some whispered, some admired
some inspired
but another day, we too,
my love and i, would stroll
this trodden hill and
recollect ... and time was still
and i was dreaming dreams

>> and then we left the town
>> forever

2.

> but she, my erstwhile love and i
> would not return to live nor die,
> instead the summons cast an eye
> on shattered dreams we now deny,
> in its splinters now the family goes
> and you and me, are me although

i traveled far, but always
with an innate searching memory
of the things that used to be,
of the birds and fields
of the same old ditch of stone
and twig and nettle seeping,
stinging through the air
and a twinkling star somewhere

perhaps i lacked a scape, as vagabonds do,
a mystic, tranquil subterfuge
bucolic, crooked, steep
where troth[1] aroused that
hidden groping eagerness
we used to talk of things that
parents, youngsters talk about
and the moon, then faraway

the old iron bridge where the train
would puff and hoot
and the stream where greasy leogs
slipped and slinked and jamjars
ruled the day,
those friable hours on the hill
now ache my somewhere heart
... there, silvie mc conn's big house

a cow mooing nonchalant sang-froid
at the gaping family clutch
his tail a weapon, dull
the midges swarm,
his tale a tale of woe
and there the maid, her cottage home ...
a list emaciated with this
twisting turn

      what had the dolmen seen?
      what had its primestone roofed?
      what tale the seanachai
      had told, today
      that stone is overturned
      as on the hill
      we tripped and heard:
      his story of our life ahead

i look behind
on a drizzling misty night
in a faraway town and
see two straying clinging lovers ...
and it makes me glad, yet sad
to hear them whisper dreams
that mingle with the rustling breeze
on primrose hill

    and a hill but mound
    and
    a mound but clay
    and
    clay but you and i
    and
    yet we dreamt ...
    and strolled along ...

[ballina, county mayo]

[1] *God of wisdom and magic, weigher of hearts*

MIDWAY

1.   after a vest-change quik-shave stay-over
       an overnight perk
       for the boss unused to long trips

> *a shave a shit and a shampoo*
> *the sailor's breakfast*
>> as my brother used to mimic

       we left honolulu

> and the hoochi-coochi gals
> with bouquet-halos on their breasts

       we looked down yesterday
       at the uss arizona from a boat
       with a glass bottom at this ship at-the bottom
       of pearl harbor's sunken-shrine:
       a museum piece of hypermnesia and rust.
       then he said, my boss

> *those bastards!*
> *those sleazy rotten bastards!*
> *those jap bastards!*
>> *remember pearl harbor!*

2.   climbing upwards in the sky
       towards morning in tokyo
       our confederate captain from waco
       texas

> *remember the alamo*

       announced:

> *gals and gents,*
> *welcome to my umpteenth trip on this route*
> *our flight path's fIxed but can vary some knots*
> *within a window based on weather*
> *and some other aberrations*
> *today you're in for a surprise*
> *with the sunrise on our side*
> *if you turn your eyes to a blip in the ocean*
> *on your right, gals and gents,*
> *you'll see the turning-point of the war in asia*

the heros of midway island
if ya'll don't mind, gals and gents,
i'm gonna break the rules
'caus soon we're comin' up dead-center
over the airstrip,
dropping down from 33 to 14000 feet
so ya'll can have a closer look.

> which he did!
> as if a tourist's taxi near an imperial palace
> not a thousand tons of steel
> slowing for the view

as the dc-10 made a nosedive
in the blue and vacant sky
i think i saw charlton heston
and those toratoratora guys
the kamikaze pilots nosediving too
a learned inspiration
for the suicide shahids
in the muslim middle east
strapped with dynamite,
strapped with semtex for sex in heaven
strapped with fantasies of kopy-kat martyrdom
lusting 72 virgins

> at least

> but suppose these shahids wake up
> to japanese
> not muslim girls, waking up in heaven
> where there may be jews too

> and what of same-sex semtex'd
> gay-shahids
> if there are only roman-baths
> in a heaven
> with catholic bachelor boys

> and what of women-shahids
>   the latest craze
> do they lust
> 72 young men just
> muslim

or japanese or jews with jewels
and golden ear-rings,
or, have second thoughts
about impure reasons
for their heavenly cause?

remember nagasaki and hiroshima
remember the gaza
strip
remember the holocaust
remember to bring your AX
don 't leave home without it
[karl maIden]

to pay for sex in heaven
to pay for their admission
to the mystery of the afterlife
before their life-and-death decision

the risks we learn from movies
religion, propaganda, indoctrination
rules that are broken
visions of surprise and hallucination
in flights of fantasy
in the delightful pleasures of death.
ah, the rub

perchance to dream and wake up
in a foreign shahid heaven
with muslims in the lower mansions
with gardens but no virgins?

through the aircraft window and its reflection
through the puffs of forming cloud
my midway photo later

like the rorschack ink-blot test

resembled a mushroom cloud
on quik-glance
apropos towards morning in tokyo

flying now dead-center
over mount fuji
looking down from the dc-10
into the inferno
of hades
of the nether world abyss
for terrorist'
shahids, muslim
or japanese or christians in ulster,
or shysters, or zionists
lusting for a heaven

       for "something attempted, something done"
        [longfellow]
       for their accomplishments and stunts

some for virgins
or bachelors
diffident to the collateral
damage

sleepy-eyed in narita
a sixty-minute bus ride
into the ginza nightlife

       and the hoochi-coochi gals
       without halos on their breasts

our meeting in shinjuku-ku
with our japanese hosts ensued
as he said, my boss
brow-beating
for the illusive purchase order
kowtowing the done-deal
       cringing

       honored friends,
       i'm proud to be your partner

       after all pearl harbor
       was yesterday,
       the hoochi-coochi gals
       last night

       remember last night!

GENERATION GAP(S)

1.   in itaewon
in the outskirts of seoul
you can see as much graffiti
as though
new york without karaoke

no cover-charge bars
and girls at their doors
babes
from the americanization
of the korean war
from the g.i. babies
left behind
now grown into grandparents

bargains are real bargains
in the emporium
even better than war time

white neon crosses everywhere
beaconing at night
as a sign of evangelical
christianity and
the western missionary
who got his foot in the door
riding the crest of the
forgotten war and
its vulnerability

even neon crosses on
mountaintops as you look
up to heaven
or travel to kwang-ju
in the south
much farther south than
north korea
where they are conditioned
to believe only
what they see on
huge billboards with
huge photos
of a leering dictator

and everywhere
student riots about graft

sometimes about the
imaginary line of the d-m-z
on the 38th parallel
separating real families
students and workers in fatigues
and the military police
forming
impenetrable shielded flanks
in close and deep ranks
in human barricades
each phalanx a 4 by 4

which i knew
because
i studied greek and latin
and the trojan wars
and shields joined together
with spears overlappin'

*come back
with your shields
or on 'em*

moving like tanks in clusters

agin' 'em

the holy pagoda
and its smell of incense
incensed repugnance
from the japanese yoke
now their tense cohort
for the soccer world cup

2.   to the east of seoul
on the eve of their shared
global goal
and a clashing competition
after a thousand years
of subjugation
by japan
straining neighborly grins
with obligatory friends
they abhor

spewing alphabetical
arguments
of k before j^3
at each other,
in each other's
face

from a common heritage,
forgotten
long before soccer
socking it to each other

for earned recognition

scuffling for position
like cutthroat movie stars
demanding top listing
in a moving-industry

of economic emulation
of historical reciprocation
of brinkmanship
of one-upmanship

for a one-zip score
for vengeance
for vindication
for

"nothing which we don't invite"
[r.w.emerson]

---

[3] *When finally the historical nemeses, Japan and Korea, agreed to co-host the World Cup, the issue became which country would have first listing*

KORINA KOREA

in designer jeans she leaves for seoul
she leaves the countryside's soft soul
behind
for city lights and opportunity
for seoular light and passion

in mini-dresses even sri lanka
draws some from their mothers' homes
and bombs beyond can't stop them

> *this was not was wrought in connaught*
> *reasons then in seamless coffins*
> *diaspora graves forgotten*

now the fad and a young girl's whim
is a young man's dream
an amen tradition
feeding a generation's omen
young girls going, young men gone
fathers dead
mothers gape at tillage rape
and pillage reasons to escape
the korean war that was meaningless

(i suppose)

rustic loss, fought for naught
fathers did are dead or not
who will care
who will care for mothers now
who will care for chonju farms?

No longer *forced* emigration from the Chonju village, young people seek their fortune and escape their heritage for the glamour of the city or abroad. Even daughters leave their mothers behind.

HONG KONG HARBOR

churning foam rising splashing
regurgitating shifts that lift like yawns
that waken the yawner, awake, now
spreads itself across a bay
uneventful as a single riseandfall
but with billions of others
like the fishes in the sea when multiplied
create an impression of powerful feed

junkets force their way against the waves
awake with something to do
violently in ownership,
exploding traffic in hong kong's harbor
exploring through created roughness
like corrugated aluminum
without its smoothness
bulldoze by like boston cabbies ignoring
red lights

casual incidents become traffic
waves busy with bouncing buoys
freighters, cruisers, sail boats
waltzing on the tossing water
not competing for space but at times
appearing to,
do what they're meant to do

other times trespassers against a whim of
casual assertiveness arrogate

puffed up rulers with space are mighty
water tillers whimsically warned
in frothing anger

now

watch your space or you'll be scuttled

CHINESE CHARACTERS

language written

cryptic, phonic, ideographic

same in cantonese and mandarin

meaning more in both or less

classy thing like eton school and rugger

or soccer ruffian itches

in uniform or britches

same but different

when my friend landed in tianjin

his airport placard name in english

umop apısdn

was held to greet him,

no one heeded

there are some characters in china,

not all pedicab peddlers

A sign in English to a Chinese might well be an upside-down sign in Mandarin. Although Cantonese and Mandarin written-characters are the same, the Mandarin spoken-dialect in Beijing may not be understood (for example) by the Cantonese dialect in Guangzhou.

DANI GIRL

1. from the 31st floor's

   revolving

   restaurant, beneath crystal chandeliers
   through the glass cage are reflections
   of a million millionaires
   who were ricepaddy threshers
   once is a lifetime of persons

   revolving

2. in china's switch to glamour
   in the stadium below:
   soccer ruffians are tottenham hotspurs[1]
   in the one sport
   where there's no respect for the civil law
   in the universal language of goal

   kicks

3. i met her in shenzhen
   dani is her english-name

   > born in 1967 what could she have done
   > when her parents were sent down?[2]

   at 27, chic, a personality of fashion
   she speaks in ways that make her eyes
   integral to syllables
   they follow every facet
   as if the surface of a baguette
   her smile matters more than 5000 years

4. of
   racing infatuation

   of
   persons closer apart than worlds

   of
   uncharted convergence

in
china's ways and hers

in
colored lights below

in
glistened waters

   surrounded by river boats
   not boat people

in
the midst of affluent skyscrapers feeling

   exotic recipience

in
a city as modern as manhattan

---

1 Celebrated English soccer team. Global football mayhem has now reached China
2 labor farms of the Cultural Revolution 1966 —76

Shenzhen: Author's first dinner date with his future wife was at the five-star
Landmark hotel.

Integral to Deng Xiaoping's road to economic reform in 1978, new cities emerged in
the special export zones. Shenzhen is one of the wealthiest of these SAR (Special
Administration Region) cities in the new China, known as China's Silicon Valley or
the Wall Street of the South China Sea. Situated just inside the mainland, Shenzhen
is Hong Kong's step-sister. The sister-cities were reunited in 1997. From a farm
population of 20,000 it has grown to a population of 10 million. The city is still
missed on most western maps.

Arriving into this satellite working-metropolis by overground subway on Friday
evenings, you are met with a quarter of a million commuters at Lo Wu station
evacuating the city each weekend like the Calgary *Stampede*. Everyone is leaving as
the officials call 500 commuter-cells every 15 seconds to the next demarcation point
at the station. The sound of each 500-person cell jogging in concert to the next
location on the platform is like a herd of buffalo. The galloping sound endures for
15-second intervals. The next 500-commuter cell follows until a quarter of a million
have passed in two hours. Only when you are arriving, as though you've been invited to
the wrong party. That is until you are met by your fiancée on the other side of the
bridge. You enter the city like Fred Astaire in the movie 'On the Beach', when only
a few people are left on earth. Only when you're through the security region of
Shenzhen, you find another ... city of the night and 9 million people who stayed
behind

INDOOR CHINA

yellow sea

1.   from seoul
just a hop and a skip and a jump
across the yellow sea

        the color of my wife's skin
        if mine is green from erin
            like the jolly green giant

to china
which i used to believe as a child
could be reached
by digging a deep deep hole
in our backyard
if you dug deeper than
australia

tianjin

2.   the cable tv tower in tianjin
taller than the sears tower
looks down
at a billion people
looking up
everyone is looking up in china
at something that is happening

        without any control of it

hoping it will be good for them
without any control of it

hinterland

3.   in the countryside the family rules
with the sincerity of family ties
kinship and ancestral worship
in the incongruity caused
by the one-child curse
eventuating little girls
to abandonment
or worse,
without uncles
or mothers hypothetically
if the rule is followed too closely

beijng

4.   beijing's buzzing too
with more bikes than amsterdam
sipping tea, playing chess, everyone
obsessed with w—t—o
and olympic delirium
as if the other stuff's forgotten
slave labor of the prison system
auctioning inmates organs
alive

nightclub

5.   discos everywhere
like the *kizzy-kizzy club*
which we thought,
my chinese wife and i
had meant a nightclub
with ballroom dancing
when we read the napkin ad
after dinner in the shrangri-la

djs playing loud-loud music loudly
with as many green guards in them
with green uniforms and
red and green pointed hats

not intimidating helmets

pointing suspiciously at something
with their batons

as soon as a dancer collapses
on amphetamines
or cocaine

or heroin from opium
the heroine from kublai khan
prompting him

spreadeagled on the disco floor

now his X a doused
kaleidoscope

you know why they're there, the guards,
and whisked away he's never seen again
or heard in the unheard sound
of a close-range silencer
unless he's paraded on a truck first
with other drug-addicts

      maybe church-
      goers too only rumored
      but you never know

through the streets
looking repentant gun-to-shaved-skull

      wouldn't you?

more effective than a penny catechism
for the impressionable
hoping it will be good for them
the public display of

      affliction

underground

6.   there's a pulse in tian'anmen
square of something gone
in the totalitarian way of things
with falun gong gone
rather fallen but not forgotten, yet
in the underground that's everywhere
      underground

chairman mao smiling leerily
      from the billboard post
      of the forbidden palace across
      in a kind of bad *feng shui*

five blocks from mcdonald's
five centuries from the ming dynasty
from the ming dynasty to mcdonalds
open, forbidden

the guards in red and green
look nervously
watching those in t-shirts

even me

particularly
if they bear an image of che guevara --
which might arouse reasonable suspicion
that you sympathize with the hallucination,
illusion, inspiration
for a notion, intuition:

" ... the imaginary gratification of
unconscious wishes"
[sigmund freud]

or even t-shirts with an image of
chairman mao, deceptively:

you are what you wear
or, what you wear may
subtly be contradictory
to the ideology
of activists in
clandestine activity

the guards like the national guard
in other countries
not much older than your child
called out
with orders to shoot the
young
if necessary

karaoke

7.   some karaoke clubs are prostitution
        dens with roman nudes outside
        like vegas statues
        in the progress that's happening

                without any control of it

        or so it seems

with one million hiv's at last count
climbing exponentially

meandering by tourist ricksha
to another *kizzy-kizzy club*
without a ballroom floor
we're welcomed
by a dozen stunning girls
barely legal for the job
lined-up to greet us
      caveat emptor or
      ... seller ...

for the experience promised
coming from the rural parts
of poverty, dreams. naiveté
with their looks
hoping it will be good for them

      without any control of it

not knowing what they might be
asked to do
in the so-called western decadence
creeping in in stampedes
of opportunity
in the culture the west can't understand
      but insists on influencing

changsha

8   shekov; hangzhou and its splendid gardens:
changsha where steve mcqueen
rammed his boat
in the sand pebbles movie

where chairman mao was born
in my wife's home town
where she graduated from,
a mao alumnum

in the museum school
i sat in the kindergarten chair
of the chairman with his proud photo
now
and his graduating tassel
at five
wondering what kind of man

56

mao was as a child
at the age of five,
at what point
a child becomes a tyrant

      a hitler, stalin, mussolini, idi amin

was it five.
or twenty-five'?
when the force of evil extirpated

"... good tortured by its own hunger and thirst"
    [kahil gibran]

or, at what point a child becomes a
respected leader

      or when the female embryo
      becomes a human soul or
      fodder

hunan

9.   the information-superhighway
conference in 1999
where i gave my paper
on cable television
on the latest hfc[4] breakthroughs
translated into mandarin.
invited by the secretary of hunan
province, the party chief,
as guest of honor
at a wedding banquet
'in honor of my wife'
and our new york matrimony

      but without my wife
      visa-stranded in new york

with ribbon-tied gifts
wrapped in red to bring home,
being hailed an
adopted son of china

the highest honor

[4] *hybrid fibre/coax*

in the culture of adopted daughters.

when all hell broke loose

at that very moment

the announcement
in the middle of his presentation
the reverberation
that we, the usa
had bombed the chinese embassy
in belgrade

at that very moment

the pandemonium
in the middle of his speech
as word was whispered
indignantly to the dignitary
mouth agasp at the atrocity
who had been praising me

and my absent chinese wife
(here in her hometown)
now naturalized american

the party chief,
in the middle of his speech
vocally vomiting in my face
now
vociferously, in mandarin,
regurgitating, retching
assuming it was intentional

the bombing by the usa

of chinese soil and people
the unmentionable prohibition,
the ww-III taboo of dr. strangelove

*how i learned to stop worrying
and love the bomb*

in the almost neverminded cold war
getting warmer
inching on the doomsday clock

in the way *we* would react
in new york on 911
not knowing what was going-on

my newfound friends walked out,
revolted, horrified, offended
with an american in their gathering

(well ... an irish-american
with dual-citizenship,
which one am i now?)

in a sickened tantrum, huffed,
as we huffed again
puffed again
bombed it all down
the chancellery
in the former yugoslavia

the plenipotentiaries

-and my translator too-

mumbling in mandarin
with only this *adopted son*
now the great satan without a clue
as to what was mumbled in the ear
secretly of the hunan province secretary

my interpreter departing too

leaving me stranded and bewildered
with ribbon-tied gifts wrapped in red
from the party chief
to take home to my chinese wife
stranded in new york
wondering what was going-on

without any control of it

zhuhai
10.   zhuhai near macao with casinos for
some not everyone
scheming to leave

shenzhen
11.   shenzhen, newest city of ten million
where the vice-premier zhu rongji
introduced me in 1996
to my wife
        now
unmapped untapped
in the special region of china's silicon valley
with the wealth of wall street and
crime

        before they cleaned up
        new york

like other cities' manipulation, exploitation,
play-the-sucker, bleed-dry
with its *windows of the world*
instant golf and disney shrangri-la
and with

        its finer folk than l.a.
        or dublin, too

the friends you've made for life
smiling through it all
the progress too
unimpinged
by what they do not know

        without any control of it

hong kong
12.   hong kong
high rise playground for king kong
and a century-plus
recovering
from england's gift of opium
addiction
is shenzhen's sister-city
both special regions now in the
two chinas

opting to be one

maybe three, or four, or five chinas
since the s-a-r's are
off-limits to their own
with special infrastructures
without a visa
for the indigenous
to visit
in their own country

guangzhou
13.   guangzhou
in the province of guangdong,
canton,
for 400 years the gateway to china,
now a gateway from china
busy with busy-ness,
the center for daily adoption
of a million little girls
        mostly

by americans at the white swan hotel

assaults your senses with tastes of
a thousand alleyway noodle shops
melding sweetness, sourness,
hotness, saltiness,
bitterness
stir-fried *chao* with
the vital essence of huoqi
the vital essence of the
vitality that's happening

        without any control of it

shanghai
14.   slithering food in shanghai
on your plate, on your table,
slipping sliding creeping crawling
as you try to fork it
faking that you like it
        tactfully
whatever it is
maybe drunken shrimp
drunk or sober
jumping
out of the translucent container

filled with rice wine
which the waitress shakes
like rolling dice

before your eyes wondering
what's inside.
incredulously you guessed
correctly
filled with living things
which locals hint
(laughing) hysterically (at you)
are tastier alive

a black and gray fast-running critter
with 6-inch feelers,
antennae-like appendages
much longer than the body
of a carrot-shaped silver-fish,
thysanurans with tail-like anal circi,
ugly as a cockroach

       or poor judd is dead in
       oklahoma

alive

lands dead-center on your plate
dillydallying

       look! my friend, he is telling you
       gobble me up, i'm delicious

       but you don't

dishes made with snake and
rat, turtle, cat
scorpion anything
that points its spine to heaven
seahorse, sea slug, starfish
flying-rodent, snakeskin.
still-wriggling sea or lake
ingredients dropped
unceremoniously into
superheated oil
as customers select their feast
from the living menu.

the day's special's for us:

'buddha jumps over the wall'

cooked cuisine so luscious
the smiling buddha tastes it
rubs his proud tummy
hops the wall in euphoria.
we sit relaxed with the soft clicks
of chop sticks
at work

> *after a full meal*
> *do not wash your hair*
> *avoid sex like an arrow*
> *avoid wine like an enemy*

mr wong

15.   mr wong arranging marriages
if you need a wife
women wanting babies
husbands wanting boys only, toys
that are made-in-china by people
unemployed in factories, now,
in the open china

xian

16.   the terra cotta warriors of xian
still alive
with 2000 individual faces
staring at the future
of china
staring

without any control of it

SILKY SIU

who are you silky siu
where are you going to
where are you coming from,

beijing, taipei, hong kong Δ?
and the dangling triangle
reverberates with a
clink-clank-clunk
good morning china

fulldeep eyes, exuberant expression
effervescent freshness
exudes an oriental welcome
to hong kong
city along the shore, english
as carnaby row

steep as the skyline
sloping like a floating
jacob's ladder of babel towers
flatter now than manhattan mirrors
looking down at night
in candlelight's contemplation
of newer chinas,
flatter, flatter
than this exotic island cube
of faces upon faces exhilarating,
junkets on the bay

fishing vessels, bobbing yachts of
white-blue-red, and red
shimmering highrise cages
veiling pagodas
glass-case malls, alley marts,
historic trams and high-tech subways

...where will you be in 1997?
said one voice to one face
nonchalant as a
silent tick-tock
cinderella's glass shoe
silky siu, where are you
going to'?

> *don't cry for me argentina*
> the singer crooned in an empty lounge
> cantonese vowels, not characters;
> words, not phonics

> > *don't flatter me either*
> > in an openness born of
> > yesterday's tomorrow
> > which china today,
> > peking, hong kong, taipei Δ?

first impression, one china,
silky siu, your name convivial
faraway silk road in marco polo-land
satiny silk in marseilles - *merci!*

sue-next-door in schenectady
the girl next door in new york,
that girl!

but, *sulky sioux?*
- don't let that happen to you!

> > what is your chinese name, silky siu
> > are you related to xiao qian, to harry wu?

with eireann torn from england,
songs were sung
a rising moon, a terrible beauty born

when hong kong hears the lunar drum
and marches to another beat
which britain now
which china now
in times and things
> > triangular Δ?

an era bred in europe
homogenized
across the wide and wide
to north and south and north
and latin south
has brought me now,
vagabond of curios, to
> > panasia

indigenous ubiquity,
alter ego quintessence
the voice and face, the eyes and eyes
the eyes of silky siu.
     where are you
when the mainland homeland,
no more homeless
is the singer and the song?

good evening china,
ladies and gentlemen;
maitre d'
with menu, missal, missile Δ

could i have your selection
    please?

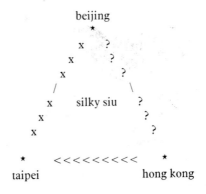

isosceles, hypotenuse? right angles? - *right!*

A smart young girl with a puppy-selected western first name, Silky, contemplates
her uncertain future at the Peak Café on Hong Kong mountain on the eve before
Britain cedes control of the colony to the People's Republic of China. Having never
travelled outside HK, from her limited western exposure, she liked the sound of the
word, silky, 'wearing' it as another might wear Mary. Enjoying her liberal lifestyle,
she wonders will it change as she now finds herself within the political triangle Δ

from the
MING DYNASTY
to mcdonald's

in eastern cultures
are hidden secrets
that elevate curiosities
of whom we are
of
        them and us

- from the
ming dynasty to mcdonald's

from the
wonders of the world to
walls of concrete,
and,
the openness of a question
        mark

                ?

from the
taj mahal to the dalai lama
and the facial sores
of an infant
amputee

from the colossus of rhodes
and cleopatra to franz kafka
and frank sinatra,
from confucius and buddha
to attila; psoriasis in africa
and inequality of birthright,

for dissertations and theses,
and
for gawking tourists

distracted in the apathy of
networked-out,
a burned-out
generation changes
with a great leap forward

- from racy shenzhen
to stodgy wuhan
and the freedom to
    strike

        (which happens today
            more often than
            you'd think
            considering
            the sheer size
            of the population
        well,
        happens, i guess,
        more than *allowed*)

stricken only
in the din of a
reawakening clamor
and an inevitable kind of
democracy

        someday

in the *open* china
becoming
        us and us

with golden arches
in an ubiquitous
buzzword-place
shattering as it ferments

the reality of mcdonald's
brings the fantasy of
ming dynasties
to the four corners
of the round earth
where the ugly beauty's
beauty only

pimples, dimples
dialogue on
worn-out sculptures
      but
      (to be sure)
      hold the ketchup ...
          huh?

McDYNASTY

- *from the Ming Dynasty to McDonald's* - is a global excursion of curiosity while scouring the past in a surrealistic search for someone today.

As an Irish-American *roaming cadillac* (figure of speech on the RC church coined by John Lennon), I encountered Hinduism, Sikhism and Islam along with the antithetical poverty and opulence of democratic India. McDynasty visits the philosophy of Taoism, Confucianism and Buddhism in communist China. In the Middle East, I developed camaraderie with Jews and Palestinians. Enjoying the panorama of Mexico, Rio, Buenos Aires, Caracas and Santiago provided a different range of vision than London, Paris, Prague and Sydney. But at day's end, the friends encountered had a sameness when the tide receded, the autumnal leaves had fallen and the clouds disappeared. On my travels I sought to discover what if anything differentiated mine from any of the smiling personas around the globe, the 'same/different, ugly/handsome, white/yellow' learned in high school as language and culture become less of a barrier.

Writers have different styles and ambience catering to their labor. As a coffeeholic I'm often found in deep absorption whiling late evening leisure hours with my pen and notebook in such unseductive settings as fast food restaurants like McDonald's around the world, undisturbed with the soft piped music and 'user-friendly' bright lights for writing, the crowd dispersed, recollecting my day's observations.

McDynasty is as much an observation of the eclectic people and places encountered along the way in evenings and weekends during overseas business trips in the cable television industry, extending as long as six weeks at a time.

As the odyssey continues, this someone in the search is now the quintessential person with the smiling eyes that tells you you're welcome to their country. You don't have to look very far to find the warmth of this welcome.

Any number of historical periods could have been selected because the polycultural fabric of McDynasty takes place in many countries. The Ming's attractiveness included: renaissance, golden era, untouchable. forbidden, words that contrast today with self-exploration, golden arches, touchable, open.

Figuratively, McDonald's refers to the Mac generation or McCulture which it helped to evolve, not necessarily the customers at a McDonald's restaurant, but they too are here. Golden arches becomes a tongue-in-cheek contrast to the golden era of the Ming. The extraordinary imaginative splendor of the worn-out sculptures and museum pieces of the untouchable and forbidden-past is contrasted with the openness and the touchable opportunity of a modern Mac generation. Dynasty has a speculative connotation of empire, fantasy, class, prestige, the unreachable, the extraordinary. The Mac generation is a nuance for the ordinary but with extraordinary possibilities for a young and class-less society with a down-to-earth sensibility. Today a different kind of succession emerges than that left behind from the wonders of the ancient world. McDynasty tries to capture the romantic with the nostalgic, the humanness, realism, aspirations and at times, the inhumanity that has always existed. The search encountered the exotic and the ordinary while the ordinary provided glimpses of an inner imagination looking out.

McDynasty, a collection of some 100 poems, takes place in six sub-continents, Asia, Australia, Latin America, Europe, North Africa, North America. One poem was written at 37,000 feet ('Contours from an Airbus') where only at that elevation the turbulent earth below seemed at peace. *McDynasty* is a story of the present with images of the past as it looks to the uncertainty of the future. The central theme is the ubiquity of the Mac generation in contrast to the Ming Dynasties and so-called museum-pieces, nice to behold, never to touch.

It seems as though I had another alien life completely detached from the hectic business schedule, as many people live two lives. McDynasty is the subliminal story seen through the other life-on-the-road, sometimes fast-paced *a la* Kerouac. It is about the global search for someone and the contrasts of realism and fantasy felt along the way.

In another, larger collection of poems, we meet the little Hindu beggar-girl with sores on her pretty face in the backdrop of the Taj Mahal. Poverty in Rio's slums, the seedy side of Copacabana. Filth behind the splendor of the pyramids of Giza, the glitz of Ginza — Tokyo's fashion area by day and clubs by night. A Ms. Universe pageant in Bangalore and the deception of cosmic surgery for gullible teenage girls. Auctioned human organs of prisoners prior to execution, female infanticide, the netherworld of the one-child policy, vultures preying over sacred cows, or … starving urchins. The open-China and Tian'anmen Square aftermath. A Latin street-hooker, a Hyde Park tart. A lap-dancer in Prague and the Copenhagen mermaid in that touchable-untouchable fantasy. A Thai stripper *working* to support her child in another country whom she may never see again. A suave Mexican cripple alert to his talent but unmindful of his disability. An exotic Saudi princess with her features concealed in a full-body veil. A singer in Manila, a flamenco in Madrid, the tango in Buenos Aires, an ex-president dancing in the jail. A Bangkok monk with his illicit cel calls, a pedophile priest, a cab con-artist, a trishaw peddler, a zealot in Cairo. The cacophany of the Sydney Opera House and the local gin-mill disco *music to the soul*. The splendor of the Alps and the Andes, looking down from an airbus dead-center into Mount Fuji. Experiencing a tornado in Oklahoma, after an air-crash in Pittsburgh, an earthquake in Mexico, a plague in India. The streets walked by Einstein, Kafka, Joyce. An IRA terrorist in Belfast (the author being taken for one en route to Tel Aviv). The thoughts of a loner in a bar, of a retiree at McDonald's. The eviction of an elderly lady, of a father. A paper-server staring-without-words 'detailing I.D.' for proof-of-delivery. The child of divorce contemplating his present as well as his future.

An elderly typewriter-writer with her PhD and fear of computers. The primrose hill in the Irish west or anywhere. The sentimentality mixed with aspirations of immigrants. The traveling gypsies in winter. An Armenian, Kurd, Muslim, Zionist. The street language and pub life of Dublin, the smile of a beggar, the thoughts of a girlfriend, the death of a mother. The smiling eyes that have no language barrier telling you that you are welcome in a foreign country, the writer's search for *Mumtaz*, Queen of the Taj Mahal.

McDynasty is also an experiment with sound, wordplay and fast paced rhythm. Some of these words have spilled-out in' a torrent during a feeling that had to be described at a moment that might not be found again. Other poems have been revised more times than Dostoevsky's forging of 'The Idiot'. Paul Greenberg, the syndicated columnist, concludes in one of his pieces: "Give me words. The kind that pound on the conscience, crack open mysteries, let light shine, or undulate across the page until the reader is hypnotized; words that sooth or alarm, inform or galvanize, open starry skies or peer into hidden recesses. The right words in the right context are like discrete droplets that rise for a perfect instant when a great wave strikes solid rock. They're fresh as now, old as the world everlasting. They rinse the mind".

The Great Wall extended during the Ming Dynasty can be seen from the shuttle. The Golden Arches can be observed by a billion people daily. In relating *McDynasty* to the Mac generation, I read a worldwide study on the recognition of popular non-fictional and fictional persons or characters. The former most commonly recognized were JFK, Chairman Mao, Elvis, Marilyn Monroe. The latter included Tarzan, Sherlock Holmes, Superman, Robin Hood and … Ronald McDonald. While the Ming Dynasty was for many of us a footnote in high school global studies, McDonald's was recognized as far away as China. It was vital to have a catchy title for this collection. *McDynasty* was solidified as I walked between a McDonald's, a Ming Dynasty restaurant and a Dynasty (China Airlines) office in Beijing adjacent to the Forbidden Palace, built during the Ming Dynasty. The Ming provided one of any number of frameworks from the lifestyles of the past to contrast the present. Dynasty, meaning 'succession', was apropos.

After the Challenger space shuttle explosion and long before the World Trade Center tragedy, the word 'vulnerable' was re-introduced into our lifestyles. The fragility of our technological prowess was probably questioned for the first time in modern history, simply reinforcing our human limitations. I saw this vulnerability firsthand in Changsha at a reception attended by the Secretary of Hunan Province. In the middle of his speech, word was reported of the US bombing of the Chinese embassy in Belgrade which had just happened. For moments I was the enemy with my American passport. As all hell broke loose, the confused and angry locals for days thought they were experiencing what we felt on 911.

from the
MING DYNASTY (1368-1644)

The Ming Dynasty was China's Renaissance. It was the first to truly open its doors to the West. It was the last of the great dynasties before the conquest of China by the Manchus. The Ming brought a period of cultural and philosophical advance during which China influenced many adjacent areas, including Japan. Great seagoing expeditions were launched to the south and west reaching the east coast of Africa. Peking was laid out in its present form, and the traditional bureaucracy was reinforced. During the Ming, the Mongols were expelled, Confucianism was reinstated, porcelain products flourished with great developments in architecture, the novel and drama. The Ming is responsible for the modern form of the Great Wall providing the greatest length as a single wall. Over 2000 miles long, the Wall is the only man-made structure on earth visible from outter space. Constructed of stone, earth and brick, its purpose was to ward off northern invaders. In practice however the Wall was best at keeping the communities locked-within as China developed its distinctive civilization. The Ming Dynasty was the Golden Era of China. It took 200,000 workers to build the Imperial Palace. Here in the Forbidden City, emperors were served by 9000 maids and 100,000 eunuchs in a complex of 800 buildings with some 9000 bays and with great courtyards of carved marble and secret gardens. Access was forbidden to all but the imperial court. The Ming is associated with: *renaissance, splendor, golden era, untouchable, forbidden.*

to ...
McDONALD'S

McDonald's represents a rags-to-riches story of a dream. Ray Kroc was a piano player and paper cup salesman of the Roaring Twenties. In middle age he founded the hamburger chain that he built from a single store into an international operation frequented by more people than any other on earth. More impressionably it is a gathering place for family or social intercourse. 'Fast-stop' is emblematic of the pace of a modern world. Yet, this pace is interrupted to stop and smell the roses, however briefly as we catch-up on the everyday events affecting us. The Little League or the Yankees game; the relief period for an office peer group contemplating their action plan; grownups discussing the inevitable changes in their lives as they learn of their parent's Alzheimer's; deadlocked lovers skimming their options; gossips and their latest conquests. This respite provides a melting pot for a society converging on itself, loosening-up, unwinding, briefly, but essentially.

JFK mingled with a crowd at a McDonald's in a popular Life magazine photo, highlighting its ubiquity in a not so dissimilar way than were it at the White House in that iconic context. Norman Rockwell made the 'All-American' image official by painting a young McDonald's crewmember serving a crowd of happy kids. Over the decades the global popularity of McDonald's has provided an image of a casual, cosmic, class-less society, sharing ideas, seeking opportunity, and, *touchable.*